I0510223

Ethereum Bible:

All You Need to Know About Ethereum

© Copyright 2018 - All rights reserved.

The contents of this book may not be reproduced, duplicated or transmitted without direct written permission from the author.

Under no circumstances will any legal responsibility or blame be held against the publisher for any reparation, damages, or monetary loss due to the information herein, either directly or indirectly.

Legal Notice:

You cannot amend, distribute, sell, use, quote or paraphrase any part or the content of this book without the consent of the author.

Disclaimer Notice:

Please note the information contained within this document is for educational and entertainment purposes only. No warranties of any kind are expressed or implied. Readers acknowledge that the author is not engaging in the rendering of legal, financial, medical or professional advice. Please consult a licensed professional before attempting any techniques outlined in this book.

By reading this document, the reader agrees that under no circumstances are is the author responsible for any losses, direct or indirect, which are incurred as a result of the use of information contained within this document, including, but not limited to, — errors, omissions, or inaccuracies.

Table of Contents

Introduction

I want to thank you for purchasing this book, "Ethereum Bible: All You Need to Know about Ethereum." The title is self-explanatory. This book is designed as a guide to help you understand, invest in and trade with cryptocurrency.

The specific focus of this book is Ethereum or Ether (ETH). If you are someone who follows the financial markets closely, you will have noticed that cryptocurrencies are steadily increasing in their popularity. The past couple of years, in particular, have seen the tremendous growth of different types of cryptocurrencies.

It is therefore unsurprising that everyone wants to figure out a way to start investing in them. Not only are they becoming more and more popular and accepted, but they are also changing the way we look at traditional financial systems themselves. The problem is that the information available about them that's crucial to understanding how they work is always presented in a complex manner. You might be led to believe that it is an incredibly complicated system that requires your own personal Yoda and years of training. While it would be great to be a Jedi, I want to tell you that this process is not as long-winded as that. You might not have experience with cryptocurrencies – and may just be someone who is looking to learn more. This book will help you in this regard, as it starts from scratch.

The focus of this book is Ethereum in particular because it has been touted a game changer in the world of cryptocurrency. Second only to Bitcoin, regarding value and popularity, many believe that it will eventually be the winner of that race. Ethereum is not showing any signs of slowing down, and perhaps it is time for you to consider the option of investing in it seriously too. This book is designed to give you the information you need and to show you how you can do this.

Through the course of this book, various concepts associated with Ethereum will be explored in greater detail. This will help you consider cryptocurrency as an investment opportunity in a more nuanced manner. We start from the basics, with an understanding of what cryptocurrency is, before moving on to focus on Ethereum. The rest of the book then gives you all the information you need about Ethereum – ranging from its history to how its trading outlook looks into the future. Explained in a concise manner, this book will hopefully give you the information you need to get started. Who knows, you might just become an expert yourself in no time!

Thank you once again for choosing this book. Happy reading!

Chapter One: An Introduction to Cryptocurrency

Any book about Ethereum would be incomplete without the mention of cryptocurrency first. The past few years have seen a great boom in the use of and the possibilities of investing in cryptocurrency. 2017 was particularly important given how quickly this kind of currency rose in popularity. 2018 looks like it is going to be similarly huge.

In all honesty, cryptocurrency is beginning to look like an unstoppable giant. It is becoming a financial system the likes of which are unimaginable; we could not have thought of this even as early as a decade ago. It has already begun changing the way we view money. Not just that, but it has also changed how we view banks and other financial systems at large. Such a boom cannot be achieved in such a short span of time without raising at least a few questions.

The focus of this chapter is going to be to help to answer some of your questions. As I mentioned previously, the focus of this book is going to be Ethereum. However, it would be useful to look at what cryptocurrency is before we jump into understanding Ethereum as a cryptocurrency and this chapter will bridge that gap by giving you some information about cryptocurrency in general.

Let me explain to you why this is important. To have a better appreciation for what Ethereum can achieve, you need to start by understanding what the world of cryptocurrency is leaning towards. This provides evidence of the larger picture at play here. Moreover, you will also be able to understand how Ethereum stands out. It has so much more to offer than other cryptocurrencies you may consider.

A better understanding of what cryptocurrency actually is will help you step away from the notion of alternative facts associated with it. Thus, through some thorough research and reading, you can come to a more realistic conclusion about the role of cryptocurrencies. You will also understand what can be achieved by using this as a financial transactional medium. We can now attempt to step away from the noise and chatter surrounding it instead.

While there are a lot of complex sentences and tough-to-understand words that can be used to explain cryptocurrency, it is honestly very simple. The term 'cryptocurrency' is used to refer to limited entries created in a database. These entries cannot be modified unless the process to modify them is initiated by fulfilling certain conditions. This should sound familiar to you by now because conventional currency works in the same manner. If both forms of currency are essentially defined the same way, the differences between them lie elsewhere. When you come to the root of it, any currency is an entry that has been verified by some database.

But what do we mean by a database? The term can be used to include a wide variety of things and in this context; we interpret it to include accounts and transactions of different kinds. The difference between currencies and cryptocurrencies, in this situation, does not lie here. It lies in the manner in which these systems operate and interact with each other. The mechanisms that govern these operations are different, leading to the facilitation of different kinds of results. Cryptocurrency networks and transactions look different from conventional currencies, and here's how.

All cryptocurrencies operate on the principle of attempting to decentralize financial systems. A fully decentralized currency would ensure that a few organizations could not have control over the entire system. Instead, it would be the community of users and the resultant network formed that would own and operate these services. This would reduce the chances of system failures and hacking.

In the case of financial systems, conventional currency systems used a centralized system of operation, such as banks. You need to trust these central systems to not exert undue influence on the currency. You do not see the same pattern with cryptocurrencies. Instead, cryptocurrencies use a network of peers to maintain and verify transactions. These peers do not need to know or interact with each other but are jointly responsible for the confirmation of transactions that take place in the system. Indeed, a defining point of cryptocurrencies that you must pay attention to is that these transactions happen anonymously. The identity of the participants in a transaction is not known to anybody but those involved.

The transaction itself, however, is a different matter. On a cryptocurrency network, the transactions are public. The available information about the nature of these transactions is used to verify them and add them to the ledger. Only after verification and approval is a transaction added to the blockchain. And this is where mining comes into the picture. I will get into the details of how mining works in a subsequent chapter in the book.

Cryptocurrency investments

Of course, all of you may have different reasons for being interested in cryptocurrency. For some of you, it may be a healthy curiosity. For some others, it could just be an interest in the world of finance and is on top of market trends. Some others may want to invest in cryptocurrency but may not know how to. There are several things you should consider when trading and investing in cryptocurrency.

To be able to make financial investments, you have to be knowledgeable about all the market trends and the way the financial systems work. Quite often, these systems are so complicated; you see yourself losing interest in learning more about them. This might even put you off investing altogether. However, with cryptocurrency, that isn't the case. It might take you a while to get started initially – but you will soon realize that it is not that hard to find your way. It ends up becoming an interesting challenge to take up. The reward potential makes investing and learning about cryptocurrencies worth it. I hope to help you on your journey towards getting proficient information about Ethereum in particular through the course of this book.

The other thing about cryptocurrencies is the potential for rewards. The fee amounts associated with conventional financial systems may seem like a necessary evil to you. However, cryptocurrency is here to show you that an alternate kind of functioning is possible too. A task as simple as buying something in a different currency leads to a hefty fee that you have to pay. These fees do add up over time and can be quite frustrating. Thus, the feasibility of relying completely on these systems does not look good. Cryptocurrency, on the other hand, lets you focus on transactions without the worry of excessive fees for exchanges. While a minimum amount is still levied, it doesn't pinch your pocket in the same way. You have to admit, over the long term, this does become more profitable for you.

Another reason to consider investing in cryptocurrencies is the fact that they are not hit by instability the same way. Like every financial system, it has its own rules in order to function. But while conventional financial systems like banks are affected by the political instability of the governance, they are involved with; this is not the case with cryptocurrency. This is because there isn't a symbiotic association between cryptocurrency and government systems. That this connection does not exist does not mean that cryptocurrencies are bad. It simply means that this financial system views instability differently, and that might be a point in its favor if it needs one.

Investing in Altcoins

Given that the first successful cryptocurrency was Bitcoin, its alternatives – or alternative cryptocurrencies in general - are referred to as Altcoins. These are successors of Bitcoin's model that are not necessarily the same as Bitcoin. Indeed, one of the significant markers of an Altcoin would be its difference from Bitcoin in a way that confers some advantage to it. The standard idea of what a cryptocurrency is remains shared by Bitcoin and Altcoins. After this point, they begin to have their differences.

People sometimes tend to worry that Altcoins will not be able to hold up in the same way that Bitcoin has. However, if current market trends are anything to consider, there is a noticeable shift toward using Altcoins. You want to get on board with that before everybody starts jumping ship. This will probably become a common occurrence as more and more people start leaning towards cryptocurrency in general.

Some experts believe that there is a very real possibility that the Bitcoin will eventually be replaced in the cryptocurrency industry. Sure, it held its own for a long period, but there are others rising too. Other cryptocurrencies, specifically Ethereum, are currently poised to take that first place in the industry in its own time. They are making the model better and are working faster to achieve this. The following chapters will explain why Ethereum is a good choice to stick with when looking into the future.

Chapter Two: Ethereum: Introduction and Background

To make sure that you understand all there is to know about Ethereum, we are going to start from the very beginning. Thus, our first step on this journey is going to be a chapter focused on introducing you to Ethereum. Who started it and why? How has it been designed and what makes it different? What are the use cases for Ethereum? This chapter hopes to answer all of these questions and then some.

The story of Ethereum

The history of Ethereum starts way back in 2013, close to half a decade ago. By this time, it had been more than five years since the inception of Bitcoin. Bitcoin was slowly gaining popularity as well as better understanding. In fact, the founder of Ethereum, Vitalik Buterin, had previously been one of the co-founders of Bitcoin Magazine. This was a source that was (and still is) dedicated to facilitating a better explanation of how Bitcoin – and cryptocurrencies in general – work. It was through founding this magazine that Buterin obtained the crucial skills necessary to understand the nuances of cryptocurrency.

The work he put into this, as well as the associated programming research that he did, eventually went into a white paper. This was the publication where he explained in detail the technical aspects associated with creating Ethereum. In addition to this, he also detailed the motivation he had behind its creation. These details were then announced at a Bitcoin conference in Florida. Around the same time, he also began working with Dr. Gavin Wood, who you might know as one of the co-founders of Ethereum. Together, they worked on their shared research project, which led to the eventual publication of the Ethereum Yellow Paper in April 2014.

I'm going to get into some detail about the motivation behind the creation of Ethereum now. I believe that this facilitates some understanding of why Ethereum works the way it does. In addition to this, you will also gain some perspective about the future of Ethereum. Through understanding these motivations, we will also be able to consider what plans the co-founders may have for the future. This is because these future-oriented goals are invariably going to be in line with the vision that they previously stated.

Buterin's goal with Ethereum was to create a space of a decentralized Internet eventually. This would be free of the restrictions and impositions that came along with a centralized system. What this meant is that anyone who wanted to be a part of the network could be a part of the network. The restrictions that might have barred them in the past would not be applicable in this space. Not only this, every party would be involved in the maintenance and functioning of the system that they were a part of. This was the idea that was first associated with the creation of Bitcoin. While there is no doubt that Nakamoto might have had a similar vision, the execution of this vision fell a little short. Bitcoin proved to be insufficient to meet all the demands associated with a decentralized space. Ethereum emerged in an attempt to fill this void that had been created in the process.

An advantage associated with the system that was being designed for Ethereum was the fact that it could operate in a trustless capacity. However, certain dangers were seen as being associated with this trustlessness that Ethereum managed to beat. For instance, in the case of rules or contracts being programmed into the system, it would not only mean they applied to everyone. It also meant that they were permanent. No exceptions were allowed in this situation. Thus, the enforcement of such agreements was equally fair to everyone. In addition to this, the involvement in the verification process meant that these rules had to be observed by the parties involved in an agreement. Through doing so, Ethereum raised the bar of what could be safely achieved within a digital space.

Another part of the motivation behind the creation of Ethereum was the space that had existed previous to it. The processing speed associated with financial systems then was one such factor. It can't be denied that blockchain technology did improve the rate at which transactional settlement occurred. However, Bitcoin's protocol had some issues with scaling which proved to be a hindrance in its future applications.

In 2014, the Ethereum Virtual Machine (EVM) changed the directionality associated with the matching in this situation. Instead of defining a specification through its implementation, it matched implementations to specifications instead. What this means, in simpler terms, is that the new system had several implementations already laid out in the beginning. Thus, a user or a developer was not restricted to a single programming language and had greater choice. This meant that you could compare the functionality of the system across platforms. In addition to this, discrepancies could also be compared more easily. Once these errors were more easily observable, combating them became that much more efficient. The factor of human error associated with a cryptocurrency vastly decreased with the launch of Ethereum. This played a large role in influencing its rise in popularity.

The Ethereum Foundation provides the current development and support required for running projects associated with Ethereum. This is a not-for-profit dedicated exclusively to this task that is based in Switzerland. Ethereum Foundation is also involved in managing the funds raised through the sale of Ether. The term Ether is the name given to the cryptocurrency token associated with Ethereum. Thus, Ethereum refers to the overall project with the overarching aims of decentralization of the Internet, not just this particular token.

Ethereum Foundation works on creating and bettering the decentralized system currently in place. Not only does it need to meet current demands, but it should also be able to adapt to future needs with a greater degree of efficiency. The mission of the foundation is to promote technology development. This development is expected to occur in more general areas aligned with the goal of decentralization, at various levels. As previously stated, Ethereum Foundation does not restrict itself only to Ether. This leads to the possibility of the development of projects that achieve the larger goal of decentralizing the Internet.

Of course, the foundation is involved in lending support to Ethereum itself. This is done by helping Ethereum develop its protocol and technology. What I have tried to highlight is the fact that the foundation does not make this its exclusive goal, which means it understands the larger picture at play here.

Design rationale

Ethereum has a high-end interface associated with it. The rationale behind designing such an interface was however associated with basic software architecture. This premise allowed for simplicity from both ends of processing. Simplicity then became one of the major principles associated with Ethereum's design process. It was something the developers strove to achieve in more areas than one. Thus, what can be understood in layman terms as a low-level concept was often used in the design of Ethereum. What they did differently, then, was picturing various combinations of these easier ideas and processes. Some of these combinations had not been considered before, lending them a unique space for their work.

Another part of Ethereum's design protocol was associated with the legality that surrounded (and still surrounds) the notion of decentralization. There are specific challenges associated with this, particularly in the area of security. In this regard, Ethereum worked differently from Bitcoin – by improving on its protocols. The manner in which data was mined and stored was changed. There were previous concerns associated with how blockchain technology could cause security risks, or eventually create the issue of space. Ethereum resolved this by treating blockchains as functional data structures. This meant the data could be stored in a highly compressed form, which solved the issue of space. Additionally, this also meant that small-scale changes would be reflected at the same time.

Use cases

Illustrating the design and use of Ethereum through using the example of specific use cases will help you understand these design details better. Such use cases are more likely to consolidate the various technologies and protocols used. Thus, you will be able to understand how these systems work as a unit, and not just how they are developed in isolation.

Given that Ethereum is a cryptocurrency, arguably, the most famous use case for it would be that of a payment system. I won't go into detail about the specific details of how Ethereum holds its value. The general understanding of how the model works comes from a comparison with the fuel model; there seems to be a degree of consensus about this. Just as the fossil fuels available in the world are limited, so are cryptocurrency tokens. Thus, in both cases, the limited availability of these resources makes them more valuable and more stable. This comparison does not indicate complete congruency between models but can be used to facilitate an understanding of how value evaluation works in cryptocurrency.

Another use case for the Ethereum blockchain relates to the purchase of gold, where it has been used. It is also predicted that this possibility of purchase may eventually extend to other precious goods and items as well. Digix developed the means to be able to purchase gold using Ether, which meant gold could now be purchased in a digital space while still considering a trustless transfer. This is useful because of all the regulations and restrictions one can circumvent in the process. For instance, the banking fees and brokerages associated with the purchase of gold can be eliminated almost completely. Tokens can be used to redeem actual gold.

A similar use case can be considered when an attempt to crowdfund too. Fundraising websites already exist in the current Internet space. However, a percentage of the target amount raised is taken by the host website in the manner of fees. Ethereum has created a space with a funding platform, but with a significant difference. Such fees are not involved in the process. Contracts on Ethereum's blockchain allow a person to transfer funds automatically. There is no third-party vendor levying different fees, changing the way crowdfunding can be achieved.

Chapter Three: Reasons to Invest in Ethereum

From talking about the basic idea, design rationale and history and background associated with Ethereum, we move to Ethereum itself. The focus of this chapter is going to be the reasons you should consider investing in Ethereum. Cryptocurrencies in general, are fantastic investments for a bunch of reasons – some of which we will consider in this chapter. However, there are some specific properties associated with Ethereum that make it that much more important to consider. When I previously mentioned to you that Ethereum stands out, this is what I was talking about. This will become clearer over the course of this chapter.

Properties shared with other cryptocurrencies

Of course, there are some properties that Ethereum shares with other cryptocurrencies. These shared properties are still good reasons to consider investing in Ethereum as well.

Preservation of anonymity

Like I previously stated, the network of peers works in a manner that ensures transparency about a transaction without revealing identities. This means that it is not possible to link a cryptocurrency account to a real-world identity. Privacy and safety are important considerations that developers think about when designing the appropriate protocol. Your identity is thus merely linked to an address, which happens to be a string of random characters that cannot be traced back to you. Referred to as a private key, no one knows about this except you. There is also no fear of hacking into your private key. This is because the degree of cryptography algorithms that go into designing this safety make it that much more rigorous. Both your identity and your investment remain safe.

The applicability of a limit

Many cryptocurrencies have a limit to the number of tokens that are issued and made available in circulation. This makes them different from traditional currencies, which are essentially "limitless." This causes the value of the fiat currency to go down over time. However, cryptocurrencies are not affected by the presence or absence of a limit in the same way. In fact, there are individuals who believe that these currencies are undervalued now and should be of greater value in the future. While the developers of Ethereum have not specified what the token limit is going to be, there have been discussions about the matter. This means a limit will be implemented sometime in the future, proposals for which are also being drawn out. The applicability of such limits is advantageous for you because you will not be caught unaware. Instead, monetary flow and supplies of cryptocurrencies can be monitored.

Transactional speed

A property of cryptocurrencies that is valued by all of its users is the speed at which transactions occur. Cryptocurrencies can process transactions much quicker than conventional financial systems can. Thus, confirmations of transactions and transfer of funds can happen in a matter of minutes. This is not affected by the location you are currently at – or what location you are trying to transfer the money to. The transactions are still processed at the same quick pace. Part of the reason this is possible is the fact that transactions cannot be reversed once conducted. This does not refer to individuals, but the system itself not offering such an option. Once transactions are confirmed, they cannot be reversed – and that's just how it is. The design of these financial networks ensures the same.

The unique position it has

Undoubtedly, there has been a decreased level of trust associated with financial systems across the world. It cannot be denied there was always some degree of discontent. However, the feeling is particularly heightened in the recent past with the financial crisis (or crises, really) that have shaken up the world in the last decade. Couple this with the fact that people are becoming more comfortable with using the Internet. You have a winner – people are looking to cryptocurrency like it may hold the key to the future, and who knows? It just might. There is no doubt that it is bringing about massive changes. How much this changes the way all of us perceive financial systems is only just beginning to be seen.

Reasons to look at Ethereum specifically

The previous section of the chapter focused on reasons you should invest in Ethereum that it shares in common with other cryptocurrencies. In this section, I will focus on what makes Ethereum unique. What makes it stand out from other cryptocurrencies? Why should consider this Altcoin in particular? If you aren't already convinced by the points raised in the previous section, these reasons will cement your decision to invest in Ethereum. Read on to find out more.

Ethereum's popularity

If you have been following current financial market trends, and those of Ethereum in particular, you will notice one thing. Ethereum is getting more popular. Over the past few years, Ethereum has managed to establish itself as the second largest digital currency around, second only in comparison to Bitcoin. This makes Ethereum a force to be reckoned with. Within the short span of time that Ethereum has been around, it has managed to convince a large number of users to invest in it. Its popularity is only bolstered by the fact that third-party applications can also run on the network.

Ethereum's increasing valuation

Again, this is a pattern you might observe Ethereum has in common with Bitcoin and other cryptocurrencies. The valuation of Ether (Ethereum's currency) has been rising over the past few months as more and more people turn to using it. There is a yearly limit to the issuance of Ether, which leads to increased demand among its users as well. This has been Ethereum's trading standard since 2016, with a limit of 18 million Ether per year. The current value of Ether is more than $350. While there is a fluctuation, it is in line with what is expected given current market trends.

Trading with Ethereum on exchanges

The accessibility that a cryptocurrency can provide makes a difference regarding its usability. If a cryptocurrency is only available on some minor exchanges (the concept of exchanges will be elaborated in the next chapter) that you don't trust, you will find it difficult to trade with that particular currency. It might even put you off that currency in general. With Ethereum, you do not face such an issue. Given its popularity at any point in time, and the manner in which it has managed to cement itself, there is an enormous availability. This increased availability of options gives you a variety of exchanges you can look into greater detail. You get to make the decision about which exchanges are more trustworthy because you have the option to do so. Users of Ethereum appreciate such an advantage.

Growing support

The number of organizations that are beginning to accept cryptocurrencies as a form of payment is increasing. While this was initially limited to Bitcoin, a growing number of organizations are allowing customers to use Ether to buy from stores as well. This would mean that your use of Ether would not be restricted to online wallets and trading. On the contrary, it is reaching out and interacting with organizations and businesses from your daily life to uncomplicate your life even further.

It also receives backing from other institutions. Take into consideration the fact that the Enterprise Ethereum Alliance is the largest of its kind in the world. It allows for collaboration on open-source blockchain technology. Here, a blockchain refers to a digital record of financial transactions that cannot be hacked or modified. At the same time, it also manages to blur the lines for the kind of institutions it manages to reach in the world. The idea is to eventually create a software network that can handle rigorous and complex business applications. Close to 200 members are a part of this Alliance, which is one that only keeps growing in number.

Growing usability

Companies and organizations that want efficient and functional networks are looking towards Ethereum. This is because Ethereum has a robust blockchain technology in place already. The presence of the smart contract also makes things significantly easier for companies to deal with, through the process of eliminating legal intermediaries. It not only saves these companies the cost of such hires, but also the time lost because of it. Ethereum has also been referred to as the "mother of ICOs" (Initial Coin Offerings). ICOs are digital IPOs (Initial Public Offerings) where cryptocurrency token can be purchased, akin to the concept of shares. The concept behind this was based on Ethereum – which created a huge momentum in its favor.

Better technology

All you need to do is go back to the time Ethereum was launched, and you will realize this is true. Ethereum was launched in 2015 to be an improvement on Bitcoin - the cryptocurrency dominating the market. Many now believe that it is going to be the currency that allows for one to push the boundaries of what can be achieved through blockchain technology. In addition to this, the code behind Ethereum is close to being what is referred to as "Turing-complete." A system is Turing-complete if it can theoretically solve every problem as long as enough memory is available to facilitate this. Thus, Ethereum might soon be able to implement every program or smart contract in such an environment.

Ethereum is faster

When compared to Bitcoin, Ethereum is also significantly faster. This is because the technology and blockchain used by Ethereum are more advanced in comparison to the former. Thus, the time taken by Ethereum when compared to its older competitor is also lesser, with its processing speed running in the degree of seconds, as opposed to minutes or much longer.

Chapter Four: Getting Started: Using Ethereum

Our next step in this guide for Ethereum is going to lean towards the practical aspects of the cryptocurrency. It is natural for you to be curious about trading with Ethereum now that you know the background behind it, how it works and why you stand to benefit from it. Investing and trading with cryptocurrency might take some time to get used to at first – but do remember that the nervousness is natural and completely okay. Don't let your worry stop you from being able to give trading at least one shot.

Obtaining and exchanging Ethereum

There are three types of Ethereum exchanges available on the Internet. Which of these you choose is dependent on what option you feel most comfortable with, and what is available in your country. Other such considerations, such as the exchange fees – also need to be kept in mind before you decide the exchange form you will be choosing.

Trading platforms

These platforms are usually websites available online that connects sellers and interested buyers. The buyer has a price that he/she would prefer that is stated as the requested price. The platform then scours through the list of sellers until one is found who matches this request and can meet the bid. This form of exchange requires no direct interaction between the buyer and the seller. This type of Ethereum exchange is probably going to be your cheapest bet when you take fees into consideration. However, the operation within such a platform is slightly more complicated compared to others.

Brokers

Brokers are websites that sell Bitcoin to you directly, but for a premium. While this will no doubt be an easy way for you to obtain Ethereum, the option is also more expensive compared to the others available that facilitate a similar process.

P2P platforms

These are websites that are similar to trading platforms, but with one crucial difference. Prospective sellers and interested buyers are merely connected through this website. It is the interaction and negotiation between the parties then involved that allows for an exchange to take place. One advantage of such sites is that they tend to support a variety of options when it comes payment methods or countries of use. However, using a p2p platform can also be risky because the interaction cannot be monitored. The person you are buying from will be anonymous to you.

Cost versus benefit considerations

Given that you have a large variety of options available for you – both regarding type and number of exchanges, you need to think about what option would be best suited for you. Sometimes, it can get quite confusing to consider all these different options. To make that process easier for you, the following is a list of considerations you need to make for a cost-benefit analysis of the best exchange for you personally.

Fees

The amount of money you stand to lose in the process of exchanging cryptocurrency is obviously an important consideration to think about. Exchanges can have various fee amounts, such as withdrawal fees, the exchange fee itself, etc. There is also a possibility that they offer some deals to make the exchange process easier for you. However, this is contingent on their policies regarding deposits, and you will have to look into greater detail for each exchange you are considering. You also need to focus on what the transaction fee itself is going to be, arguably the most important fee in this equation. Once you have calculated how much you will have to give to get a good exchange, you might be one step closer to finalizing an exchange itself. Information regarding fee amounts of an exchange should be available to you on the exchange's website.

Locations served

This seems like it might be a bit obvious, but you will need to look for an exchange that works in your country of residence. In addition to this, you might benefit from an exchange that allows you to use your home currency without having to deal with foreign exchange in the first place. Some exchanges tend to be restricted by geography and serve a very specific locale – the user base of such exchanges is also restricted in these cases. It is also possible that the full feature-list of an exchange is not made available to you in your home country but is available for other countries. You will want to look into this before choosing your Ethereum exchange.

Background and verification

The process associated with background and verification may be slightly irksome for some. However, you cannot deny that such verifications serve an important purpose; they do help in reducing the instances of scamming to some degree. You might then benefit from choosing an exchange that requires you to verify your identity before being able to use the exchange. While the process may take a couple of days, you will gain full access to your account and will be able to use it as necessary. You have the added benefit of knowing you tried to minimize the instance of scamming.

Options for payment

While this might seem like a mundane consideration to make, it does become a matter that irks some people over others. For instance, there are some exchanges that do not facilitate for you to be able to pay the way you wish to. You will benefit from having a variety of options such as wire transfers or card payment to choose from. Your convenience does matter in this situation. Again, regarding the fees levied, it is possible that some exchanges charge greater amounts for payment to be done in the manner that you want it to. This is something you should look to avoid. Also, try to look for options that facilitate quicker payment routes.

The exchange's reputation

You should be able to verify an exchange's reputation fairly easily. All you need to do is look for what the users of the exchange have to say about it. Do the experts in the area have a preference for an Ethereum exchange? What do the negative reviews say – are these things you should have considered as well? Look for answers to these questions using a quick search, and you can be more convinced about which exchange you want to settle for.

Ethereum wallets

To be able to store your Ether as safely as possible, you need to use a wallet. For this purpose, this section of the chapter is going to discuss the different options you have available for Ethereum wallets. You need to remember that private keys in the case of trading with any cryptocurrency are very important – once you lose your private key, your Ether will also be lost forever. This is where the dual nature of decentralization comes in because you will not be able to ask anyone to recover your key. Thus, you need to keep your private key in a safe place. This is where the concept of a wallet is introduced. There are a variety of options available for Ethereum wallets: desktop, web, hardware, and paper. Which of these you choose depends on what you think is more convenient and secure for you. Find the right balance, and you will have found the wallet of your dreams!

Desktop wallets

Desktop wallets, as the name suggests, are those that run on your computer or laptop. You will have to download an Ethereum client, which is the term used to refer to a copy of the whole blockchain. Your option of client varies depending on the programming language of your choice. The download in itself will take a couple of days – and the duration is going to increase in time as Ethereum grows. This is because the wallet needs to be constantly synced with the client.

Mobile wallets

Lighter versions of the desktop wallets, these can be downloaded more easily and connect to the network quicker to facilitate transactions. They obtain their name from their usability on a smartphone. While this is a convenient option to consider, as it will take up considerably less time and data, safety can be an issue here. You will have to ensure that the nodes send you accurate information about the transactions.

While desktop and mobile wallets depend on an Internet connection for their use, it is also possible to use other wallets. This method of storing private keys is referred to as cold storage. Given that the device is detached from the Internet, your information cannot be easily hacked. Thus, such devices are recommended for those who have large holdings of Ether.

Hardware wallets

This is an option that you can consider if you don't use Ether too frequently. These devices are small in size and can be detached from the Internet. At the same time, it is also possible for you to sign transactions while still being offline. The operation of a hardware wallet is similar to that of a deposit-box.

Paper wallets

This is a system that might require you to use a real deposit box. Paper wallets, as the name suggests, involve the idea that you can type or handwrite your private key on a piece of paper. This paper is then stored in a safety deposit box. As this is a cold storage option, it is safe from the vulnerabilities of hacking.

Do remember, though, once your private key is lost – it is lost forever. This means you should seriously consider the option of creating several copies of the key. After doing so, store them in different locations, so you have an option to fall back on, in case you lose one copy.

Difference between public and private keys

One crucial difference you will want to understand is that between public and private keys. Similar to credit card numbers that serve as identification of where money needs to be sent, cryptocurrencies allow you to create such identification numbers as well. This would facilitate the transfer of funds effectively. When considering cryptocurrencies, there are two types of keys (identification) that you need to know about. These are the public key and the private key, both of which are represented by a string of alphanumeric characters. The cryptography that links these keys is also already in place.

To be able to spend Ether, you are required to use your private keys to confirm wanting to sign over your funds. This works similar to a password that confirms you want to go ahead with the transaction. On the other hand, your public key is what will be sent to others. If other people want to send Ether to you, they will need an address to send it to – so the transactional operation can be completed. Sharing this will allow others to send money to you.

Chapter Five: Mining with Ethereum

The next step in learning more about Ethereum involves an understanding of what mining is. The term itself may sound very strange and foreign to you. I'm sure you first image might be that of you deep down in a cave, digging away at something. Well, the reality is slightly different compared to that. By the end of this chapter, you will be able to understand better the details associated with mining. The necessity of mining, how it works, and other aspects will become clearer to you. Mining is essential for the functioning of the financial network, and you will see why.

Like it has been stated previously, cryptocurrencies operate on the basis of wanting to decentralize financial systems. This means that the technology associated with it allows you to be able to achieve this. When you have a financial system with no external regulators or gatekeepers, there does need to be a substitute in place for this. Verification of transactions in the network needs to happen in some form, so one can be assured that fraudulent transactions do not take place.

This verification is what is referred to as mining, in the context of Ethereum. What miners do, is use computational capacities and cryptography to be able to decipher and control every block that is newly added to the blockchain. While this might sound difficult, the process simply involves computers guessing a huge number of options until the "right" answer is obtained for verification. These attempts are referred to as a Hash.

You might wonder why a miner would even bother with something taking up so much time and computational capacity (translating to power usage). This is because Ethereum rewards miners for going through this trouble in the form of Ether, which is also then processed by the network. If two miners are working to solve the same block, it is obvious that one of them will solve it before the other. In this case, the miner who didn't solve it as quickly simply abandons work on that block and moves to working on the next block instead. The algorithm associated with this is referred to as the "proof of work" algorithm. The reason this trial and error process works is that checking a Hash does not take up much regarding computational power, even though it does eventually add up when one is trying to find the right Hash.

What you make as a miner thus depends on how much computational power you have – and how lucky you get with any given block. It is these factors and the power costs that you need to take into consideration if you are thinking of mining.

In the case of Ethereum, the processing time for such mining is close to 15 seconds. The algorithm Ethereum's network uses (proof of work) is essentially the same as the one used by Bitcoin. But like I previously mentioned, Ethereum networks process things at a much quicker rate. Thus, the difference between the two lies in the speed of the network. While Ethereum blocks take 12-15 seconds to be mined, a block of Bitcoin would take 10 minutes. In addition to this, the difference between these two also lies in the amount of reward available. Bitcoin's reward for mining seems to be going down by half every four years. Finally, with Ethereum, the algorithm used for mining – is slightly different from Bitcoin regarding its memory requirement. Ethash requires more memory than Bitcoin does, and you will need to consider this when thinking about what devices to get to facilitate mining.

Getting started with mining

There are different ways to go about mining depending on your level of technical expertise. If you think you have good technical skills, that's great – but even if you don't, you don't need to worry. There is an alternative available that you can use. You should try to choose the method that works best to your advantage. The difference between these two methods lies in the allowance of optimization. Cloud mining is an option for those who are not comfortable with their level of technical expertise. On the other hand, if you do have a technical background, you will be able to carry out optimizations on a mining rig (a computer system to mine tokens) yourself. What kind of optimizations are we talking about here? Simply put, you're looking to maximize your mining while minimizing the amount of energy spent on it.

Choosing the right hardware

To start mining and get the best out of the process, you will want to start by considering the best options you have available for hardware. If you are setting up your mining rig, you will need to look for options that have a high Hashrate (simply put, greater processing capacity) but taking up as less energy as possible. You don't want to end up setting a mining rig when you end up spending more in energy than you manage to get out of mining. Examples of GPUs you can consider for this include Radeon RX 470 and Radeon R9 7990. Pit their Hashrate against the energy costs you will face – and you will conclude what GPU is best for you.

In contrast to the GPU, a CPU is not that important to the mining process – this is because mining works on graphics power. However, that does not mean you should buy the cheapest CPU model available. CPUs do serve their function in helping you set up the mining rig, so keep that in mind and choose wisely. You also need to have a high RAM to sync with the blockchain the first time around. For this, you need to have a RAM of 4 GB or more, often perceived as being the minimum account required for an Ethereum miner.

Now, it is also possible that you want to consider mining, but do not have the technical expertise that is required for you to be able to set up the mining rig. Like I mentioned, that isn't a problem either. You will still be able to mine Ether, just by using a different route. Cloud mining is becoming more and more popular each year, particularly in the field of business. Countries that have higher power costs also benefit from using such cloud mining services, as it minimizes the amount that is lost in the process.

Using a cloud mining service with Ethereum is quite easy. The simple concept behind it remains the same. Somebody who can provide mining "rents" their computational capacity to you. You enter a contract with this mining provider for a predetermined amount of time and a certain Hashrate. The initial setup is simply limited to this contractual agreement, followed by connecting this to your wallet. You will eventually get Ether in your wallet. Cloud mining providers such as Hashflare are available for this purpose.

Choosing the right software

After getting the right hardware in place, the next step is obtaining the right software for the mining rig. Described below are a few examples of mining software that you can consider using.

Geth: The original software developed by the Ethereum team is called Geth. If you are going to work on your own and without the help of cloud mining hardware, this is probably your best bet. Geth works on the command line (*cmd*) for this process. This means you need to have some level of experience working with *cmd*. The lack of a GUI (Graphical User Interface) means you're better off having some level of experience before choosing this option. The software itself, however, is not very complicated. It not only allows you to mine but also creates your wallet.

Claymore: Claymore is one of the most popular software used for mining. It is touted to be easy to install and use by many users of the programs. Compared to other software in the market, there are many extra options available to tweak the software to suit your convenience. Additionally, the software gives you the option of extracting two coins simultaneously. User experience dictates that this has the possibility of giving you an extra 10% in income.

Other mining software is available in minimized forms for you to be able to use on your computer. These aren't directly related to the mining rig you might consider but instead give you a smaller version of Ether. The GUI of such simpler software leads to ease of use – and this will mean you can start using them almost immediately. However, such software often has its charges. An example of such software would be Minersgate.

OPTIONAL: Joining a mining pool

Once you have set up your Ethereum mining rig, you have the option of working with other miners in a group. Such groups are referred to as mining pools. This is not a step you need to take if you don't want to. The basic principle behind this is the fact that individual Hashrates are not enough to solve a block in time. Thus, combining Hashrates with other parties would help you solve the block quicker. After a specific block has been solved, the reward for the block is divided fairly – not equally. This would mean that the Hashrate you contributed would determine how much reward you get. Examples of Ethereum mining pools include Ethereum pool and Nanopool.

Connecting your wallet

I've previously elaborated on what an Ethereum wallet is and how you can make it. Well, you need to use it in this step by connecting your mining rig (or cloud mine) to your Ethereum wallet. This would facilitate the transfer of the Ether eventually mined directly to your wallet once the process is done.

Chapter Six: Trading Strategies with Ethereum

Now that you are aware of the basics of trading with Ethereum, this chapter is going to go into the details of trading. This should help you in deciding how to be smart about your investments. It is one of the more practical aspects of dealing with Ethereum, so you need to understand it properly. After all, you do want to learn more about Ethereum because it has the potential to be profitable for you – why let that go?

When you are trading Ether, there are two types of possible strategies that you can consider employing. The first of these strategies is referred to as active trading. This talks about the concept of trading Ether several times within the same day or week. Thus, you are actively involved in the trade of Ethereum and do not keep the tokens with yourself for very long. In this sense, you are operating from a short-term perspective. The idea is that you need to be able to smartly predict and work through market fluctuations.

The second kind of trading strategy refers to the buy-and-hold strategy, which works in the longer run instead. Here, you are in no rush to sell your coins as soon as you can. Instead, you hold on to Ether through the more minute fluctuations that occur across a day or week – sometimes going into months. Once the right moment is available to you, you sell the Ether. To achieve this, you need to keep an active eye out for what is currently going on in the world. Responding to larger political or financial events at the opportune time can be very advantageous for you.

Active trading strategies for Ethereum

Each kind of strategy you may consider has its kind of advantages and disadvantages. Weigh these against each other carefully to decide which would work best for you. As mentioned above, In the case of active trading, you only hold Ether with you for a short period. This can range from a few minutes to a few weeks. This would mean that the amount of work you put into monitoring market fluctuations and changes will be that much greater. You need to constantly look at the market to see when the volatility will benefit you. While this time spent monitoring might seem like a lot to you, do realize that you now have the opportunity to gain that much more.

The amount of time you will need to commit to be able to trade actively can be a lot. Over time, this can get stressful. So, to choose this strategy, you need to be confident about your ability to analyze and notice patterns. In addition to this, more importantly, you need to have the time to commit to the process. Before you choose to go down the active trading route, ask yourself whether you can do all this.

Also ask yourself what you are looking to gain from the current situation, for instance, what gain percentage you're looking at, or the practicality of spending that much time trading. Think about how frequently you want to set profit targets for yourself. This will give you an idea of how much time and energy active trading is going to take from you.

There is a simple rule to be followed when you are active trading – buy low, sell high. What this means is that you look at a time when the price of Ether is relatively low and buy tokens then. Once the price of Ether goes up, you sell it. You can look at the fluctuation yourself to decide – looking at its exchange rate will tell you how well it is doing. Your other option is to use trading tools that let you set alerts for buying and selling. Thus, you specify what rate you would like to buy at – then decide what rate you would prefer to sell at – and mark those. This tool will then be able to alert you when these numbers are reached. However, this service tends to be a paid service. While you might need to lose some money, think about what you stand to gain. If you're – well, actively – active trading, it becomes quite useful to have trading tools like these.

If you would like to save money and work towards trading through personal practice instead, that is still an option. If you are analytical, you will notice that each cryptocurrency has its trading patterns. This means that as long as you put in observation and analysis from your end, you will be able to implement strategies that work best for you. You might initially feel more comfortable using someone else's trading strategy. You can continue to do this until you figure out what pattern works best for you.

To best notice these patterns, you could follow the following strategy. Divide the day you are looking at into timeslots of, say, ten or fifteen minutes. Use this to create a plotting chart to track the highs and low of Ether trading. There are trading platforms that help you make such charts. Once you look at some charts, you will see that a pattern emerges. Some times of the day are better for buying compared to others, while a similar idea is true for selling Ether as well. Specific days of the week might be showing more upward movement compared to others. Follow the trends of the market closely and respond as quickly as you can to it.

Rest assured, there will be more than one instance during the day when trading will be beneficial to you. Once you figure out the pattern, it won't be difficult to choose a time that is convenient for you instead. Similarly, you will notice that some strategies you employ may work, while others won't. You will gain experience through these trades. You will also see that this experience will help you make more intuitive decisions about which strategies aren't working. This will allow you to modify it to make it better. Set goals for yourself – this will help you decide when you want to sell.

Buying and holding with Ethereum

Buying and holding is a strategy that refers to a long-term strategy that works exactly as the name might imply. You exchange a certain amount of money to obtain a certain amount of Ether, and you store it in your wallet. Decide on specific conditions that need to be met for you to sell Ether. This can be Ether reaching a certain value or a period. After this, simply put, you hold the Ether in your wallet. Achieving this goal can take a few months, or even over a year – which is why it is referred to as a long-term investment. This will free you from the immediate volatility of the market and confers benefits for you in the long run.

If past trends are anything to go by, Ethereum and Bitcoin are leaders in their market. While some degree of fluctuation is to be expected, the value of Ethereum is not expected to drop too much anytime soon. Those who bought ETH in its early days are now benefitting hugely from the profits made over this period. Similarly, several long-term investors are looking to join in and benefit from this as well.

One of the most significant advantages of the employment of this strategy is that you save a lot of time and energy. As all you are required to do is buy and hold, you will no longer have to track the market for everyday volatilities. You also don't need to concern yourself with immediate news related to the financial market. Another advantage of choosing this strategy would be the fact that you lose less money in transaction fees, simply because you don't actively trade as much.

Consider the buy and hold strategy if you aren't very confident about your technical skills related to the market. The simplicity associated with the strategy will put significantly less stress on you. You will not be required to meet immediate time-bound obligations or stare at charts constantly to figure out patterns. This is a good option to consider if you want to secure an investment in place for later. Given that the popularity and reach of Ethereum are increasing with it, it is highly likely that your investment will pay off in the long run anyway. However, do make sure you have a safety cushion to fall back on. If your strategy does not work to your benefit, how much are you comfortable with losing? What is your contingency plan if such a situation arises?

Selling Ethereum after using mining pools

If you choose to join a mining pool, you will be expected to provide an address where the rewards for mining will be sent. It isn't wise to send these rewards directly to an exchange-based wallet. There is a possibility that the public address will change over time. Thus, to sell ETH after mining, you need to complete one more step. Set up another wallet, maybe a local one, to receive these rewards for mining. Once you do so, you can transfer these tokens wherever you wish, and sell them if you want to.

Chapter Seven: Trading Outlook for Ethereum

In the final chapter of this book, we are going to look at how the outlook for Ethereum looks currently, particularly from the perspective of trading. To put it succinctly, the trading outlook for Ethereum looks good. The cryptocurrency is showing tremendous growth and potential. In addition to this, developers are Ethereum are looking to push the boundaries of what can be achieved using cryptocurrencies. The icing on the cake is the idea that Ethereum is touted to replace Bitcoin eventually. Even if it does not manage to do so, this is a strongly positive response to have to the growth of Ethereum. Those of you who are looking to invest can rest easy knowing the same.

Expert opinion about Ethereum

To understand what lies in Ethereum's future, the best source of information you can probably get is from the co-creator of Ethereum. Through the course of several interviews regarding the future of Ethereum, its co-founder, Buterin clarified that plans are being made to scale the project. He aims to improve the current model of Ethereum to test how far it would be possible to push the boundaries of functionality. Currently, the barrier for such attempts tends to be a loss of stability. Through the course of several test runs, he hopes to be able to achieve a balance between the two. The ideal state achieving functionality even as the system remains stable as a result.

In addition to this, he spoke about the necessity of getting information out to the general public. The prevalent lack of understanding about cryptocurrency tends to skew the public perception about it. Many people pass off cryptocurrency as being either too complicated or too volatile, to be taken seriously. However, Buterin hopes to work with his organization to make the public better aware of the work that is currently being done by Ethereum. Doing so is not just going to convince more people to start trading using ETH. It might also achieve the larger goal of achieving greater acceptance for cryptocurrency (and decentralization, more generally) in the public.

Trading outlook

Ethereum was launched close to three years ago and has shown a great amount of growth. The newness of the currency has also made it more volatile. Thus, making short-term predictions about the price of Ether can be very difficult. To give you some perspective, the value of Ether can fluctuate close to 20% in a single day. The very next day, it might regain this. The first quarter of 2018, in particular, has shown a lot of volatility, going as high as $1,440 or as low as $550. Thus, making price predictions from a short-term viewpoint does not seem like it might yield the best results. It might be better to follow long-term predictions about what is to be expected instead.

There are predictions that Ethereum might touch the $2,000 mark by the end of 2018. Given how much growth it has shown in the year of 2017, this is not a large leap to make. Conservative estimates keep this number at around $2,000 – while bolder predictions say it might even come close to $5,000. The demand for the currency, in addition to the number of currency tokens (ETH) currently in circulation, will have a role to play in influencing this rise.

There is also a real possibility that the competition between Ethereum and Bitcoin will get even stiffer. In the last few months (as of April 2018), Bitcoin has been steadily losing its market share to Ethereum. In the same period, the share of money invested in Ethereum went up by four times. Given that 3-4 months can make such a large difference, it does remain to be seen what this means for Ethereum possibly beating Bitcoin by the end of this year. While Bitcoin is popular with some governments, the option of smart contracting that is available with Ethereum makes it a popular choice for companies. This even led to the formation of the Enterprise Ethereum Alliance, facilitating the growth of Ether even further.

When considering a larger perspective, it does seem like the positives outweigh the limited negatives that currently exist. For instance, Ethereum is working on its problem of scalability even as Ether becomes more popular. Thus, the realists among us can be assured that the next few years do look good for Ethereum.

Conclusion

This brings us to the end of this guide to Ethereum and Ether (ETH). True to its name, this was a book designed to assist you in your quest to learn everything there is to know about the cryptocurrency. Thank you, yet again, for choosing to purchase this book. I hope that you found it helpful in gaining the information you needed and that the book changed the way you see financial systems now.

A new investment can always come as a challenge – exciting and scary in equal amounts. It is understandable if you are nervous about investing in cryptocurrencies. Take a moment to applaud yourself for taking that important first step towards conquering your fear. Through the very act of buying and reading this book, you have decided to give your consideration deeper thought. That, in itself, is part of the battle won. Congratulations on achieving that!

The idea behind the design of this book was to provide some insight into all areas of Ethereum. This is why the information provided in the book ranges from more theoretical aspects (such as the history of Ethereum) to practical considerations (like a choosing a wallet for Ethereum).

I hope that getting such a well-rounded perspective will make you feel confident about the investment decisions that you choose to make. Once you start investing, you will notice that you can approach these strategies with the clarity that accompanies practical attempts. You will soon be aided by your experience, in addition to your intuition and gut feeling. This might take you a while to get used to, but don't worry about that! We all figure out trading and finances at our own pace – it is our journey and ours alone. For this journey, as dramatic as it may sound, good luck!

Thank you again for downloading this book!

I hope this book was able to help you .

Finally, if you enjoyed this book, then I'd like to ask you for a favor, would you be kind enough to leave a review for this book on Amazon? It'd be greatly appreciated!

Sources

https://99bitcoins.com/best-ethereum-exchange-review-comparison/

https://blockgeeks.com/guides/what-is-cryptocurrency/

https://blockgeeks.com/guides/what-is-cryptocurrency/

https://blockk.co.uk/ethereum-mining/

https://blockonomi.com/how-to-mine-ethereum/

https://gaiatrader.com/top-5-reasons-invest-ethereum/

https://github.com/ethereum/wiki/wiki/Design-Rationale

https://investingpr.com/ethereum-price-predictions-for-2018/

https://www.coindesk.com/information/how-to-use-ethereum/

https://www.cryptocompare.com/mining/guides/how-to-mine-ethereum-the-easy-way-an-ethereum-mining-contract/

https://www.ethereum.org

https://www.forbes.com/sites/panosmourdoukoutas/2018/02/16/what-could-lift-bitcoin-ripple-ethereum-and-litecoin-prices-back-towards-new-highs/#4648b8956476

https://www.independent.co.uk/news/business/news/5-reasons-to-invest-in-ethereum-a8120101.html

https://www.intertrader.com/blog/watch-youre-trading-ethereum

https://www.vitalik.ca

www.ingramcontent.com/pod-product-compliance
Lightning Source LLC
Chambersburg PA
CBHW070520220526
45467CB00002B/756